The Saxons

Saxons first came to Britain as mercenary soldiers and later, with other Germanic invaders, seized land from their employers after the collapse of Roman rule. The newcomers and their kinfolk set up kingdoms, among them Essex, Kent, Mercia, Northumbria, East Anglia, Sussex and Wessex. Rulers were laid to rest in impressive royal tombs, some tantalizingly revealed by modern archaeology. Over the next 500 years, warrior-kings forged a unified kingdom of the 'English' in which, by the 900s, art, literature and scholarship were flowering. Great monarchs such as Alfred and Edgar ruled with the support of a vigorous Church and powerful earls, and were backed by fiercely loyal soldiers battle-hardened in war against Vikings, Scots and Welsh. The Norman Conquest of 1066 imposed a new order on England, but Saxon roots ran deep and the Saxon legacy, not least in language, proved permanent.

The Saxons Arrive

The Romans finally let Britain go in the early 400s AD. After 400 years of fighting, building, ruling and civilizing, Roman troops sailed away, back across the Channel to save the core of their Empire. Britain – the northern outpost – was left defenceless to face the same challenge that had called the imperial army back to Europe: revolt and attack by Germanic peoples.

Cast outside the Empire, southern, Romanized Britons fell prey to the raiders and pirates who had plagued their lands for over a century. Northern Picts joined Scots from Ireland who stormed the west coasts, while east-coast tides landed boats from the North Sea, carrying seafarers seeking work, land and a new life. In the end, this tidal onrush proved overwhelming, and turned Roman Britain into Saxon England.

Looking back at their history, the Angles, Saxons, Jutes, Franks, Frisians and other Germanic settlers who mingled to comprise the 'English' recorded their arrival in Britain in *The Anglo-Saxon Chronicle*, a yearly summary of events:

ABOVE: *The Romans wave farewell, a scene imagined by a 13th-century artist who pictured the departing legions not in Roman armour, but in medieval dress.*

410 The Goths broke into Rome, and never since has Roman ruled in Britain.
418 The Romans gathered all the gold hoards in Britain; some they hid in the earth, so that no man might find them …
446 The British sent men over the sea to Rome and asked for help against the Picts, but they never received it. They sent then to the Angles …
449 Then came the men of three Germanic tribes: Old Saxons, Angles and Jutes.

RIGHT: *The King Arthur of legend accepts homage from kneeling knights. This romantic figure, illustrated here in a 14th-century French manuscript, is far removed from the Romano-British war-leader who battled to stem the incoming Saxon tide.*

FAR RIGHT: *A map drawn c.AD 950 shows the Roman forts of the Saxon shore, built to guard the coast and repel Saxon pirates from across the North Sea.*

The story's bare bones mask a more complicated, gradual link between Saxons and Britons. The newcomers were mercenaries, lured by Roman gold to fight off raiders – often fellow-Saxons. When, by ad 410, the Roman army left their island altogether, desperate British leaders continued paying Germanic warriors to bolster their defences, but the hired help took over, seizing land they had been paid to defend.

Flooding in their old homelands (north Germany, Denmark, Jutland) may have forced the Saxons westwards, swelling the number of arrivals in Britain. The Britons rallied briefly under such leaders as the legendary King Arthur, but fighting throughout the 500s left British-run territory confined to Wales, the far west and isolated kingdoms such as Elmet (Yorkshire). The last major British 'resistance fighter' was Cadwallon, killed by Oswald of Northumbria in 633.

Their kingdoms established, the Saxons settled to farm – and to fight among themselves. Threatened with loss of their land to Vikings in the 800s, they held fast under the leadership of Wessex kings to found a united nation that in the 11th century survived absorption into King Cnut's Scandinavian empire. But the end was near. At Hastings in 1066, after 600 years of controlling the land they had made their own, Saxon rule in England was swept away. The Saxons themselves were not.

ABOVE: *A section of* The Anglo-Saxon Chronicle, *written around 1046. The last paragraph describes Alfred's defeat of the Vikings at Edington, Wiltshire, in 878. Probably begun at Alfred's command, the* Chronicle, *written in Old English, was compiled at different centres.*

ABOVE: *Saxon foot-soldiers felled by the chain-mailed might of the Normans. This Bayeux Tapestry scene records the defeat of Harold's army at Hastings in 1066 and the Norman victory that signalled the end of Anglo-Saxon England.*

Royal Saxons

'In this year two chieftains, Cerdic and his son Cynric, came with five ships to Britain ... and they fought against the Britons ...'

Entry for 495, *The Anglo-Saxon Chronicle*

In 519, the same Cerdic and Cynric are said to have founded the royal line of Wessex (the West Saxons). Other Saxon kingdoms also traced their ruling dynasties back to the chiefs of invading war-bands – or even to the pagan gods. Brothers Hengist and Horsa – Jutes who by tradition took control of Kent around 450 – were among those with the Germanic god Woden planted at the root of their family tree. The *Chronicle* goes even further: 'From this Woden sprang all our royal families ...'.

Early Saxon England was full of kings. Fighters foremost, they were strong enough to win and keep territory – and plunder for their men.

ABOVE: *Ethelbert, king of Kent (565–616), from a 13th-century genealogical roll that includes a history of the kings of England.*

Tightly knit, closely related tribal groups chose their king (*cyning*, 'man of family') from leading warrior ranks. They ruled from barn-like wooden palaces, or halls, leading small armies of followers bound by the 'loyal unto death' code of Saxon warriors.

War between Saxons and Britons and among Saxons themselves resulted in smaller kingdoms being engulfed by larger ones. Kent, pre-eminent under its famous king Ethelbert (560–616), later came under the overlordship of Mercia and Wessex. Sussex's small kingdom, ruled by 'South Saxon' kings until 773, fell to Mercia and then Wessex. East Saxons in Essex, having absorbed the Middle Saxons (Middlesex) by 600, were taken over by Mercians.

Outstanding leaders won fame and power. Such were the bretwaldas, 'Britain-rulers', among them the Northumbrian kings Edwin (616–33), Oswald (634–42) and Oswy (642–70), whose royal halls at Yeavering in Northumberland have been identified. Here, the ruler would stay once or twice a year, hunting by day and feasting at night, before moving on to the next royal hall with his retinue of loyal followers. At its peak in the 700s, Northumbria stretched from east coast to west, from the River Humber up to the Firth of Forth.

ABOVE: *This family tree of King James I (1603–25) shows his apparent descent from the Roman Brutus, legendary founder of Britain, and from Woden, king of the Nordic gods. Many Saxon royal dynasties claimed similar ancestry.*

RIGHT: *Saxon lords and kings entertained their warriors in the mead hall, where they feasted, drank, heard heroic tales of past glory and distributed gifts in return for loyal service.*

4

East Anglia, kingdom of the Angles, covered Suffolk ('south people') and Norfolk ('north people'). Its most famous kings were Raedwald (c.615–25), possibly buried in the Sutton Hoo (Suffolk) ship, and the saintly Edmund 'the Martyr', slain by Vikings in 870. From its Midlands heartland, Mercia later expanded into the Thames valley and north to the Humber, while Wessex spread from its 6th-century Hampshire stronghold north to the Thames, east into Sussex and west up to the River Tamar. Mercia's remarkable King Offa (fl. 757–96) was the first to call himself 'king of the English', but it was Wessex's royal line that produced the kings who would rule a united England.

ABOVE: *The severed head of the East-Anglian king Edmund, (855–70). Venerated as a Christian martyr, his slaughter by marauding Vikings is said to have been a particularly bloody sacrifice to their god Woden.*

LEFT: *Detail of the ceremonial 'whetstone' or 'sceptre', with a bronze stag at the top, found at Sutton Hoo and now in the British Museum, London.*

The High and Low

'The very peoples of the English, their kingdoms and their kings, fight among themselves.'

Alcuin (c.732–804), monk of Northumbria and adviser to Charlemagne

Shunning the crumbling walled towns of Roman Britain, Saxon farmers preferred to lead a rustic village life. But while farmers ploughed, warrior kings fought one another for supremacy. Most Saxon kings ruled with pagan ferocity, even after converting to Christianity, and the loyalty code that demanded revenge for spilt blood kindled frequent feuds.

In 626, Edwin of Northumbria was attacked by a would-be assassin from Wessex. In revenge, the king invaded the southern kingdom, killing 'five kings there and a great number of people'. Edwin later fell in battle (633) against Penda of Mercia, who then devastated Northumbria, slaying its king (Oswald), before being butchered in turn by Oswald's brother Oswy. Yet family loyalty had its limits, and kings could be ruthless in eliminating rival relatives; Edwin's family fled to Gaul after his death, rather than trust the goodwill of Oswald, a Christian but still a Saxon.

Dynastic violence echoed through the annals of Northumbria. Aethelred, king in 774, was driven into exile but his successor Aelfwold was killed in 788, and Osred (son of a previous ruler) became king. Two years later, Osred was overthrown by Aethelred, who had Aelfwold's two sons murdered after luring them from sanctuary in York Cathedral. Osred, again seeking the throne, was betrayed and killed by Aethelred – who was assassinated in 796. Such ferocious feuds were the counterpart to loyalty alliances cemented between lord and followers at feasts in hall as the deeds of dead warriors rang out in song.

ABOVE: *Illustration from the Aelfric Pentateuch, a manuscript in which biblical scenes are illustrated by figures such as these Saxon peasants, reaping and working with contemporary farming tools; from St Augustine's Church in Canterbury.*

ABOVE: *Fragment of a 7th-century bronze from Sutton Hoo; this enamelled escutcheon from a hanging bowl is decorated in Celtic-style scrollwork around a central area set with millefiori glass.*

BELOW: *The king and his minister, with sword of justice, sit in judgement at the city gates. Law-making and law-enforcing were among the prime functions of a Saxon ruler.*

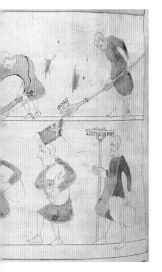

Kings ruled with a council (witan) of noblemen (thegns) and clergy over a society ordered by rank: warriors, craftsmen, farmers (ceorls) and slaves. But it was possible to rise: a ceorl who owned 'five hides of land of his own, a bell [possibly hung in a tower] and a burh [fortified place] gate, a seat and special office in the king's hall' was entitled to the rights of a thegn.

Each person knew his own worth, or *wergild* (man-tax), the compensation payable to a victim's family if somebody killed him. Death money, also used to make redress for other crimes, varied according to rank and from kingdom to kingdom. In 7th-century Kent, noblemen (*eorlcund*) were rated at 300 shillings; freemen at 100 shillings. The king's *wergild* was highest of all – six times that of a thegn in Mercia. Sutton Hoo's 7th-century ship burial reveals the rich splendour of an early Saxon warrior king, whose trade links stretched across the seas to Scandinavia and mainland Europe.

ABOVE: *Stone-carved figures on a Saxon font in Toller Fratrum Church, Dorset.*

LEFT: *Orion the hunter, drawn on his (dotted) constellation. He is portrayed as an Anglo-Saxon thegn, standing with raised sword at a porticoed entrance.*

BELOW: *Cutting corn at harvest time. Under the eye of the reeve, peasants slash the ripe stalks with sickles, then pitchfork the crop into a waiting cart. Illustration from an Anglo-Saxon calendar, c.1030.*

7

Warring Saxons

'… the iron blade was adorned with deadly, twig-like patterning, tempered with battle blood … the ancient treasure, the razor-sharp ornamented sword …'

from *Beowulf* (c.1000)

Saxon society was based on a code of honour, kinship and loyalty. A warrior shared the spoils of victory in battle, but willingly gave his life for his lord. It was thought shameful to leave the field unscathed, once a leader had fallen. Fleeing foes were pursued and slaughtered, to exact vengeance for slain comrades.

Armies were small – a fleet of five ships might land only 200 or so men, and a king's retinue might not exceed 50. Though Saxons rode horses, they fought on foot, and battles were bloody hand-to-hand trials of stamina, lasting until one side was either slaughtered or fled.

Favourite Saxon weapons were the sword and spear, and later the long-handled axe. Spears, held for thrusting from behind the protection of a wooden shield, were hurled like javelins. The longest shafts were over 2m (6ft) long and ended in various kinds of iron-cast points. Slaves were not allowed to carry spears. Any slave found with a spear was punished by having the shaft broken across his back, and since an ash-wood spear-shaft was extremely hard to break, this meant a severe beating.

ABOVE: *Warriors from the 8th-century Franks casket, a box of panelled whalebone decorated with both biblical and pagan Scandinavian scenes. Its carvings include runic inscriptions and give useful details of Saxon dress and weapons.*

ABOVE: *A sword handle found in Fetter Lane, London, in the 19th century. This 8th-century hilt, fashioned from several pieces of silver, has a plain pommel (top), in contrast to the interlaced snake spirals, typically Saxon, on the grip.*

ABOVE: *A decorative detail from the warrior's helmet found at Sutton Hoo, reconstructed from surviving flakes of tin-bronze foil. The scene shows a mounted warrior riding down a mail-clad enemy, who stabs the horse as he falls. The style displays Swedish connections.*

Honour in defeat

The warrior code was enshrined in Old English poetry, where heroic deeds are celebrated even – or perhaps especially – in defeat. *The Battle of Maldon* describes a real-life skirmish in 991, when a band of Essex men confronted Viking invaders at Maldon. With foolhardy bravado, they let the enemy cross the causeway from their island camp to meet them. The English lost the ensuing fight, but the bard praises their leader Byrhtnoth for his noble heroism, and those warriors who fulfilled their loyalty pledge by fighting to the death for their lord. In the words of one, 'Thought shall be the harder, heart the keener, courage the greater, as our strength ebbs.'

BELOW: *A Saxon spearman, in conical iron helmet and protected by his shield, prepares to meet the enemy. The ash spear could be used in close combat or thrown as a lance.*

ABOVE: *Northey Island in the Blackwater Estuary, site of the Battle of Maldon.*

The battle axe, as carried by King Harold's bodyguard at the Battle of Hastings, was formidable, but the most prized weapon was a sword. Saxon swords were crafted with patient skill by iron-smiths, using a technique known as pattern-welding to twist iron rods together. This produced a herringbone pattern on a two-edged blade about a metre (3ft) long. The sword, sheathed in a wooden scabbard lined with sheep's wool and covered with leather, hung from a fighter's belt.

A warrior's protection was his wooden shield and iron helmet. Among the few helmets to survive is that from Sutton Hoo, magnificently fashioned for the king buried with it. Another helmet, from Northamptonshire, bears a boar crest. Boars also feature on the Sutton Hoo helmet, reflecting the animal's special place in Germanic and Old English lore. The Roman historian Tacitus commented: 'This boar avails more than weapons or human protection; it guarantees that the worshipper [of the Mother-Goddess Nerthus] is without fear even when surrounded by enemies.'

ABOVE: *An iron axe-hammer found in a Kentish grave. Dating from the 6th century, this is an extremely rare find from Saxon England. The decorative detail suggests a specialized weapon, not a tool.*

Saxons at Home

Saxon farmers created a new landscape, felling woodland to clear fields that they ploughed in strips using a simple ard (or scratch plough) and a heavier ox plough with a mould-board that could turn clay. Families kept sheep for meat and wool; cattle and pigs for meat and hides, or other useful items such as horn or bristle. Summer's harvest yielded wheat and rye (for bread), and oats for animal feed and porridge.

Vegetables included purple carrots, parsnips, small cabbages, peas, beans, onions, leeks and wild roots such as burdock. Honey, for sweetening, also produced a potent drink called mead (the *Beowulf* poet recounts warrior high-jinks in the lord's 'mead-hall'). Apples made cider, or were eaten with other fruits such as plums, cherries and berries. Fish bones from refuse pits are evidence that Saxons enjoyed perch, pike, trout, herring, salmon and eels, along with various shellfish including oysters, mussels and cockles.

The big house of a settlement, hamlet or village was the lord's hall (later the manor house) and next in size was the church. Ordinary Saxon homes were usually of wattle (woven twigs), wooden planks or, sometimes, turf or stones. Stout wooden doors were shut with latch keys of iron or deer antler. Inside, a fire burned for warmth and cooking, its smoke filtering out through the thatched roof and eaves.

ABOVE: *A group of Saxons. Men wore tunics and breeches; women, loose-fitting dresses with long sleeves.*

LEFT: *A late 6th-century drinking vessel made from a horn of the extinct aurochs, or wild cattle. Found in a princely burial at Taplow, Buckinghamshire, this would have been a prized possession, used for ceremonial drinking in the great hall.*

A farmer urges on his oxen. Two-wheeled wagons were the basic vehicles for heavy cartage, and such simple, robust carts were widely used to cope with the rough tracks that served as roads.

Candles made of tallow (animal fat) might flicker in the gloom, but most Saxons regarded sunset as bedtime.

A picture of Saxon villagers themselves is deduced from grave remains and manuscript illustrations. They seem to have been tall – women's skeletons commonly measuring 170cm (5ft 8in) and men's up to 180cm (6ft) or more. Female hair was probably worn long, tied or plaited, while razor finds suggest that some men shaved their chins, although most grew moustaches. Ankle-length dresses for women were of wool or linen, worn over a linen under-tunic. Men had knee-length tunics over baggy trousers bound puttee-fashion with linen bands. Pins and brooches acted as clothes fasteners.

Although poems portray women as mourning widows, abandoned wives, or noble hostesses plying guests with mead, Saxon family life is rarely mentioned. Stark evidence comes from the personal possessions with which most Saxons were buried. Any wooden or leather toys in children's graves have long since rotted away, although a boy's grave at Great Chesterford, Essex, yielded a shield, spear and the bones of a dog, presumably a favourite pet.

BELOW: A golden disc brooch from Monkton, Kent, set with garnets and shell. A brooch's distinctive shape and decoration can reveal if it was worn by a Jute from Kent, an Angle from East Anglia or a Saxon from Sussex.

LEFT: A shepherd watches over his sheep in a rather idealized Italianate landscape, from an English manuscript illustration of the early- to mid-11th century. Though small compared to modern breeds, sheep became an important commodity in Saxon England.

LEFT: Honey provided the only source of sweetening for foods, and the basic ingredient for mead. There survive examples of Saxon beekeepers' charms, spoken to persuade a swarm of bees to settle into a new home.

Art and Letters

'The wave, over the wave, a weird thing I saw,
Thorough-wrought, and wonderfully ornate:
A wonder on the wave – water became bone.'

Riddle from the *Exeter Book* (c.1000), left to Exeter Cathedral by its
first bishop, Leofric, who died in 1072. The answer: ice.

Few Saxons were literate, despite Alfred the Great's efforts to educate
his people, but a rich oral literature passed down the generations and
some was later written in manuscripts by Christian monks. Scribes, illustrators and
bookbinders created volumes of rare beauty and value (such as the Lindisfarne
Gospels), which proved so tempting to Viking raiders.

ABOVE: *Women playing
harps, from a biblical
manuscript. The sound
would be familiar in great
Saxon halls, where scops
(minstrels) plucked small
harps or lyres as they recited
the ancient heroic songs.*

Religious books were in Latin, but Saxon poetry and prose were written in the
Old English dialects that people spoke. Anglo-Saxons also had their own system of
letters, called runes. These 'secret letters' of mystery and power were used for
inscriptions, spells, riddles and charms. 'Sing that same charm into the man's
mouth and into both his ears and into the
wound before he puts on the salve' are
directions for use with a herbal
healing paste mixed from old soap,
apple juice, egg and ashes.

Saxon poetry sprang from the
heroic tales of Germanic tradition –
of voyages, monsters, gold, greed,
heroism, darkness and death. There
are battle poems, Christian poems
such as *The Dream of the Rood* [Cross]
and sad poems of exile. Much Saxon
poetry has a plaintive, sorrowful tone.
It does not rhyme, but uses descriptive
phrases ('foamy-necked floater' for a
boat, for instance) and is driven by
alliteration (words starting with the
same sound). The style lasted until
rhyming poetry was introduced
by the Normans.

RIGHT: *The Annunciation, from the
Benedictional of St Aethelwold, a
richly illustrated collection of blessings
which Aethelwold, Bishop of
Winchester (963–84), ordered
written by the scribe Godeman.*

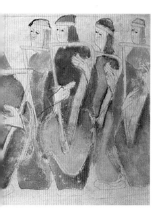

LEFT: *A glowing abstract 'carpet-page' from the Lindisfarne Gospels. Probably produced for Eadfrith, Bishop of Lindisfarne, the Gospels display a fusion of Celtic, classical and Byzantine elements that distinguish Hiberno-Saxon art.*

BELOW: *A piece of replica embroidery from Sutton Hoo illustrates the style of floor covering possibly used in the halls of Saxon kings.*

Story-poems were sung to guests in the lord's hall by minstrels called scops, who plucked a harp or lyre while reciting the words. Song-singing like this occurs in *Beowulf*, most famous of all Saxon poems, which – though written down around AD 1000 – was composed earlier, possibly 700–750, and describes events in early 6th-century Scandinavia.

The finely wrought wordplay of Saxon poetry has its visual match in exquisite jewellery produced in Saxon workshops. Tantalizingly few examples survive from grave finds such as Sutton Hoo, or rare discoveries like the 'Alfred Jewel', but they display intricately designed abstract ornament typical of Saxon metalwork. Just as delicately produced is the embroidery for which Saxon women were famed throughout Europe. Besides priceless church vestments, they also stitched the Bayeux Tapestry.

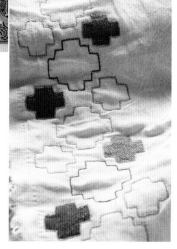

RIGHT: *A gilded silver mount with biting animal head (perhaps a wolf), and runic inscription – probably part of the binding of a scabbard for a seax, an Anglo-Saxon weapon and the root of the Saxons' name.*

ABOVE: *The opening lines of Beowulf. This great Saxon epic poem tells the tale of a dragon-slaying hero and embodies the virtues of the Saxon warrior caste: loyalty to kith and kin, generosity, courage and stoicism, tinged with doom and gloom.*

Lament for a lost world

'Wondrous is this wall-stone. Ruined by fate, the fortresses have fallen; the work of giants is no more ... where in past times, many men light-hearted and adorned with gold and jewels, flushed with wine, shone in their war armour and looked on their treasures ... there the baths were hot in its centre ...'
Extract from *The Ruin*, an Old English poem about a ruined city, thought to be Roman Bath.

Pious and Pagan

'... terrible in shape ... long necks, thin faces, yellow complexions, filthy beards, shaggy ears, wild foreheads, fierce eyes, foul mouths ... twisted jaws ... scabby thighs, knotty knees, crooked legs, swollen ankles, splay feet, spreading mouths and raucous cries...'

Description of wicked sprites seeking to invade St Guthlac's lonely fenland cell

Newly arrived Saxons lived in a world haunted by supernatural beings – giants, dwarves, witches, elves and trolls. Walking in fear of the unknown, they carried amulets or charms to ward off evil and sickness, and cast runes to seek signs. Their gods were those of the northlands: Woden (Odin), lord of magic and leader of the 'Wild Hunt'; the storm god Thunor (Thor), with his thunderbolt hammer; Tiw, god of glory, honour and warriors; and Frigg, goddess of childbirth. Nerthus was the Earth Mother and Harvest Queen; Oestre, goddess of dawn and spring; and Rheda, the winter goddess.

The Britons displaced by the Saxons were largely Christian, a faith kept alive in Celtic areas by saints such as Patrick, Columba and Aidan. Nobody had yet tackled the pagan Saxons, but in 597 a mission from Rome arrived in Kent. Its leader, Augustine, although fearful of the Saxons' terrifying reputation, nevertheless took his message to King Ethelbert, whose Frankish queen Bertha had brought her Christian chaplain with her to Britain. Fearing witchcraft, the king insisted on an open-air meeting, but afterwards allowed Augustine, first archbishop of Canterbury, the use of an old Roman church in his capital. Raedwald of East Anglia, another cautious convert, permitted a Christian altar but only inside an older pagan temple. Christian bishops followed suit, often siting churches on pagan sites.

Death and burial rites

Saxons buried or burned their dead. People of high rank were buried beneath mounds, with 'grave goods' – glass, pottery, wooden bowls, copper cauldrons, miniature buckets, knives, spindle whorls (drop weights), jewellery and weapons. Graves also contained boar tusks, wolf and beaver teeth, perhaps worn for protection, and even cowrie shells (traded across Europe from the Indian Ocean), pierced Roman coins and fossil belemnites – all valued for their magical properties.

ABOVE: *A 7th-century beaver-tooth pendant, possibly worn as a charm against toothache.*

RIGHT: *The Norse god Thor, wielding his hammer as he stands before a thundercloud.*

When Ethelbert's daughter married Edwin of Northumbria, her Roman priest Paulinus completed a rapid conversion of the northern kingdom, becoming the first archbishop of York. Yet Saxons were slow to give up their old traditions and, on Edwin's death, Paulinus fled back to Kent. His Northumbrian church all but died out, but Celtic missionaries were also at work in the north, planting monasteries: Columba at Iona, Aidan at Lindisfarne, Benedict Biscop at Jarrow. The great churchmen of Northumbria also included St Cuthbert (c.635–87), St Wilfrid (634–709) and the Venerable Bede (c.673–735), who spent his life at the monasteries of Monkwearmouth and Jarrow. In 663, the Synod of Whitby was called to decide which form of Christian tradition – Celtic or Roman – should be used throughout England. It decided in favour of Rome.

By the time of King Ine of Wessex (688–726), it was decreed that 'a child is to be baptized within 30 days; if it is not, 30 shillings compensation is to be paid'. When Offa of Mercia died in 796, he was acclaimed a leader of European Christendom, on equal terms with the Pope and Charlemagne of the Franks, soon to be crowned Holy Roman Emperor. The people of this 'king of the English' were for the most part Christian.

Saxons United

'I took my gladness in the cry of the gannet and the sound of the curlew ... in the screaming gull ... he who ... suffers few hardships in the city, little believes how I often in weariness had to dwell on the ocean path. The shadow of night grew dark, snow came from the north, frost bound the earth; hail fell on the ground.'

From *The Seafarer*, in the *Exeter Book*

ABOVE: *King Athelstan enthroned, in an initial illustration to a 14th-century English manuscript in the British Library. Althelstan, having made himself supreme in Britain, married his daughters to European princes.*

BELOW: *Saxons ships, a 19th-century engraving from an early manuscript. Single-masted and steered by an oar at the stern, the vessels have dragon-carved prows. A head, possibly cut off in battle, provides added ornament as well as a meal for seabirds.*

Saxons were seamen: 'The hard night watch in the prow of the ship was often my duty ...' says *The Seafarer* poet. They lived close to the sea, wrote about it and travelled across it. Settlers in England traded with Europe and beyond through a complex system of land and sea routes. Sandwich was a busy cross-Channel port; Southampton (Hamwic) and Ipswich (Gipeswic) were important trading points too. Bede calls London an 'emporium' – meaning a market for merchants from many lands. The Strand was then a beach onto which sailing ships were hauled. York (Eoforwic) was another important trade centre.

Ruled by a powerful king like Offa, Saxon England seemed secure; yet it was during his reign that a new threat came from the sea. In 789, while Offa was negotiating the marriage of his daughter to Charlemagne's son, three Viking ships landed in Dorset. In 793, Vikings struck again: 'heathen men miserably destroyed God's church on Lindisfarne, with plunder and slaughter', in the words of *The Anglo-Saxon Chronicle*.

From Charlemagne's court in Europe, the English scholar Alcuin of York wrote to the king of Northumbria, expressing horror at the news but also warning of divine retribution for a slack people's sins. The English had little respite for 'slacking' during the following century as their kingdoms struggled to fight off growing waves of invaders from Scandinavia and Denmark. The large Viking army that landed in 866 threatened the very

ABOVE: *A silver penny of Eric Bloodaxe, last Viking king of York (947–54), who ruled as a client of the Wessex dynasty. After his death in battle at Stainmore, Viking York was absorbed into Saxon England.*

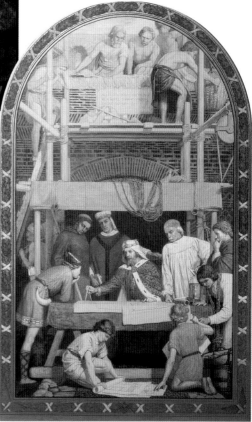

LEFT: *Danes besiege Canterbury, in a 13th-century stained-glass window from the cathedral. Vikings attacked the city in 1011, drunkenly killing the archbishop, their prisoner, when he would not promise ransom.*

ABOVE: *King Alfred checks the plans for refortifying London, after winning the city back from the Danes in 886. A painting by Harry Mileham, 1907.*

existence of Saxon England. Vikings overran Mercia and East Anglia. Only Wessex was left. Here, Alfred became king in 871 (a year in which nine battles were recorded), survived near-disaster and emerged from the Somerset marshes to win a key victory at Edington in 878.

Alfred let the Vikings settle in the east (the so-called Danelaw). He fortified towns (burhs), organized the militia (fyrd) into a standing army, and built a navy of large ships to guard the coastline. He issued a code of laws, adopting from custom 'those which seemed to me most just' to deal with such matters as the blood feud or wergild fee, and giving equal justice to English and Viking alike. He regained London, a Mercian city before its capture by the Vikings, and made Mercia his ally.

Alfred's vision was of a nation united not only by military victory but by faith and learning. He wanted his people taught and led by educated priests, translating the *Pastoral Rule* of Pope Gregory and sending a copy to every cathedral. When Alfred died in 899, a new England was forming.

Alfred's descendants built on his foundation. Under Edward (899–924) and his sister Ethelfleda ('Lady of the Mercians'), Athelstan (924–39) and Edgar (959–75), English power grew. By victory at Brunanburh over Scots, Welsh and Irish Vikings, Athelstan secured Saxon England, and in 959 Edgar confirmed Saxon supremacy by accepting the homage of Welsh and Scottish kings.

Late Flowering ... and Fall

Edgar's court at Winchester was among Europe's most brilliant; not for nothing did admirers call him 'the Magnificent'. These years saw the high point of Saxon culture, especially in art and architecture. Prominent in the king's council was the Wessex-born Archbishop Dunstan, who reformed the monasteries, rebuilt churches and sent missions to Scandinavia. For part of his early life a hermit at Glastonbury, Dunstan was also a skilled scribe, musician and metalworker – making bells and organs. He ended his life as a teacher at Canterbury's school.

Saxon kings were guided by their council of wise men, the witan, comprising Churchmen and lords. In a sense, this council was a forerunner of Parliament, although less 'democratic' than the Viking concept of the Althing or communal meeting. Just as Saxons shaped the landscape and created the shires, so their civil structure of villages, towns, Church and justice fashioned the English way of doing things, and their achievement still underpins much of Britain's modern administration, over a thousand years later.

BELOW: *Harald Hardrada, king of Norway, dies in battle against Harold of Wessex at Stamford Bridge, 1066. This later medieval picture shows a clash between knights on horseback, not the footslogging epic of the Saxon battlefield.*

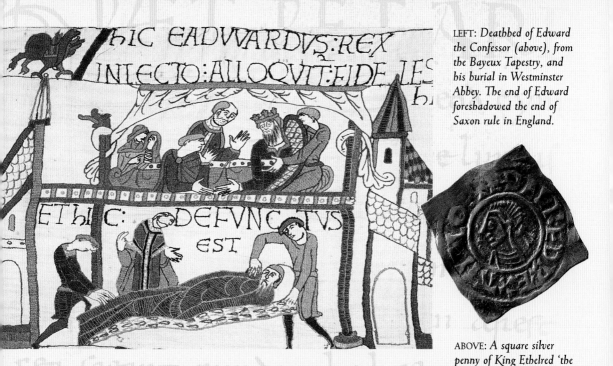

HIC EADWARDVS REX INLECTO ALLOQVIT FIDELES

ET HIC DEFVNCTVS EST

After Edgar, however, the flowering lost its bloom amid furious family squabbling. 'There was no chief who would assemble forces, but each fled as he might,' declared the *Chronicle* for 975, two years after Edgar's death at the age of only 32. Ethelred ('the Unready') gave silver in vain to fend off Viking armies led by Danish kings intent on conquest. In 1016 a Dane, Cnut, became king in England, which formed part of an Anglo-Scandinavian empire.

Neither of Cnut's vicious sons reigned long, and under Edward the Confessor (more Norman than Saxon), the great earls of England – Leofric of Mercia, Siward of Northumbria and Godwin of Wessex – played off a deadly power-game between English, Norwegians and Normans. When Edward died in 1066, Godwin's son Harold was the witan's choice as king. Harold had all the Saxon warrior virtues, crushing a Norwegian invasion force at Stamford Bridge in 1066. But – eerily echoing the Saxon poets who warn of misery and loss after happiness and cheer – victory was followed by disastrous defeat.

HIC MILITES EXIERVNT DE HESTENGA

William of Normandy won the day at Hastings where, in truly heroic Saxon fashion, Harold and his brothers were left dead on the battlefield amid their loyal bodyguard. Unbroken Saxon rule in England had ended, though the English remained Saxons still. Saxon people and their ruling Norman landlords began a slow merger, grafting a new nation onto deep and ancient roots.

Places to Visit

Bewcastle Cross

BATH, Avon

Victoria Art Gallery
Saxon coins from Bath mint

BATTLE, East Sussex

Battle Abbey
Site of the Battle of Hastings, with audio-guided battlefield walk

CAMBRIDGE, Cambridgeshire

Corpus Christi College
Houses the oldest manuscript of the *Anglo-Saxon Chronicle*

Museum of Archaeology and Anthropology
Small display of artefacts from Saxon period

CANTERBURY, Kent

Canterbury Cathedral
Seat of English Christianity

Canterbury Heritage Museum
Saxon glass and jewellery, including Canterbury Cross

St Augustine's Abbey
Intact 7th-century walling

St Mark's Church
Saxon font; church in constant use since 6th century

CARLISLE, Cumbria

Tullie House Museum
Artefacts from the Saxon period and a replica of the Bewcastle Cross

CHESTER, Cheshire

Chester Cathedral
Relics of St Werburgh, 8th-century Mercian princess

Grosvenor Museum
Anglo-Saxon coins

DEERHURST, Gloucestershire

Odda's Chapel
Saxon chapel

HOLY ISLAND, Northumberland

Lindisfarne Priory
Ruins of the Benedictine priory built near the site of the Saxon monastery

LONDON

British Museum
Displays Saxon treasures including those from Sutton Hoo

Museum of London
Collection of artefacts from Saxon times

Westminster Abbey
Founded by Edward the Confessor, who is buried here

NEWCASTLE-UPON-TYNE, Tyne & Wear

Museum of Antiquities
Artefacts from the Saxon period, including the Falstone memorial stone, crosses with runic inscriptions, tools, jewellery and pottery

Sutton Hoo at sunset